Light of Hope

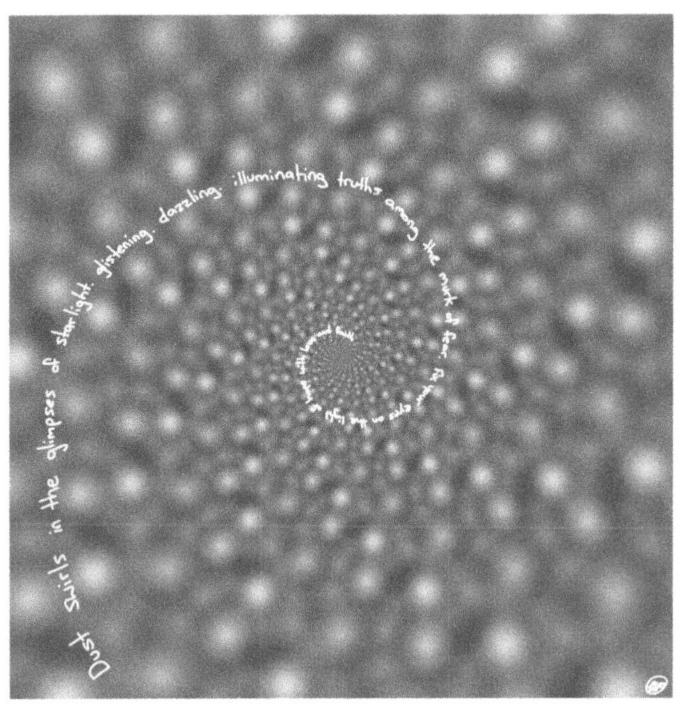

A collection of poetry, prose and art by refugees and their friends

Special Edition

Light of Hope

ISBN 13: 978-1-4717-1416-0

Editor - Emma Major
Cover Art - Emma Major

Introduction

This book brings together poetry, prose, paintings and photographs created by 32 people from all over the world.

Half of the creatives who have generously provided their work are refugees, waiting to find a place to call home.
The rest are friends and supporters of refugees,
raising awareness of the refugee crisis,
campaigning for justice for everyone who has fled their home
and providing practical help in a variety of ways.

All the money raised from the sale of this book
will be donated to the charity
Phone Credit for Refugees.

"Phone Credit for Refugees and Displaced People supports asylum seekers and refugees separated from their families by war and conflict. We provide mobile phone top-ups so that they can get in touch with their families, communicate with support agencies and stay safe.

We are a humanitarian response organisation set up by ordinary people — volunteers who give their time freely to help refugees feel safer.
It is volunteer led and run, with no full-time employees.
All money raised is used to provide phone credit, with a very small percentage going to provide outsourced infrastructure support."
https://www.pc4r.org/

A Child by Islam

(مات الصغير)

طفل يعاني قسوة الحرمان   يشكو الذي يلقاه للرحمن

قد مات والده وماتت أمه   والأهل قد صاروا بلا أوطان

أمسى يتيماً تائهاً ومشرداً   طفل بلا دار ولا عنوان

يمشي على ذاك الرصيف مردداً   ياموطني عذراً لكل هوان

لم نلق بعدك يا دمشق لروحنا   سكناً أضعنا اليوم كل أمان

طفل يتيم والحياة تذيقه   كأساً من الآلام والأحزان

وأتى الشتاء على الصغير بقسوة   برد وجوع فيه يجتمعان

الجوع يقرصه بكل قساوة   والبرد أتى مثلما العدوان

متوسداً صندوقه في رقة   فلعله يعطيه بعض حنان

الموت داعبه روحه بمحبة   هيا إلى روضٍ من الأفنان

نم يا صغيري نحو أهلك إنما   تلقى النعيم بجنة الرضوان

نم نحو والدك الشهيد فإنه   قرب النبي وأصدق الخلان

مات الصغير من الشتاء وبرده   من جوعه من قسوة الحرمان

مات الصغير ولا عزاء لأمة   رضيت بكأس الذل والخسران

A child suffering harsh deprivation
He complains to God about the pain he faces
His father and mother dead
And all the parents have become without homelands and without countries
Become an orphan lost and homeless
A child without a country or address
He walks on that sidewalk and says,
Oh my country, what happened?
I have not found a home like Damascus, a home that embraces my soul
Today I lost all safety
An orphan child and life continues to give him a lot of suffering and pain
And winter came to the little one harshly, with cold and hunger
Hunger cripples him with all its cruelty, and cold is like aggression
Hiding in a box hoping to give him some tenderness
Death played with his soul lovingly
Come to eternal paradise
Come on, my little one, towards your mother, where you will receive bliss in Heaven
Come to your father, the martyr, for he is near the prophets and the chosen ones
The little boy died of winter and cold
From hunger and harsh deprivation
The little boy died without consolation for a people who were satisfied with humiliation and loss

This poem, it means to me a lost homeland and a deprived child.
A cold tent with no roof or walls ......
These words express my sadness for the children of syria,
The children of the war, who were and are still dying
from deprivation and cold.
I hope that peace will prevail in my country and all the countries and that every child in this word sleeps in his bed next to his mother without fear, injustic or deprivation without war without blood, peace then peace and then peace for the children of my lost country!.

Islam is in year 10.
She came to County Durham, England with her family on the Syrian Resettlement Scheme.

The Women of War by Becky Morrisson

From the grandmother huddling in fear in her padded coat
Trying to keep up appearances
With her smart handbag.
To the scared woman holding a baby so tightly
As if she would never let go.
To the woman curling into herself in a warm blanket.
As she finally gets to safety.

To the crying woman in a hijab relieved to escape.
To the politician who knows she is hated more as a woman
To the diplomat with her perfect hair scared at putting a word wrong as it may cost lives.
To the Duchess showing her colours in a small badge worn discretely
where royalty normally stand back .

We need to be proud of all these women.
Our women of war are joining those over time historically and around our world.

Faceless and timeless
The women of war fighting
In different ways.

Refugees by Julia Hill

Fleeing hurriedly,
Fear propelling, panic rising,
Heart pounding, sounds piercing
Ripped from familiarity
Lives wrenched from normality
Cruelly torn away from family
Disbelief this is their life story
Desperate for safety
Facing vast tides of uncertainty
Engulfing waters a bitter reality

... Peace perfect peace...
Is my cry of prayer O refugee -

In your leaving and your arriving
in your resting and recovering
and your weeping and heart grieving.
In your breathing and your sleeping
in your waiting and your watching
in your gratefully receiving and your talking
in your shaking and your settling
in your hoping and bravely living
... peace perfect peace ...
Peace to fill your heart,
to carry you through these days
This is my prayer for you O refugee

Looking for Hope

by Emma Major

From darkest places
Life can seem impossible
Keep looking for hope

Generosity
Overflows for Refugees
Spring tide of welcome

Do you see the two silhouettes of people either side of this sea cave?
I see one person ready to listen to the other, with light of hope between them.

Song For A Refugee Child

Poem by Merry Cross, Painting by Dave Lupton

Your family's not from round here
They came from far away
You walked and walked and walked and walked
But weren't allowed to stay
In some spots where you stopped to rest
And tried to sleep the night
Although the stars were overhead
And daytime brought more fright.
So dreams did not come easily
And often you were cold
For food ran short quite early on
And your Mum thought you bold
To beg for just a piece of fruit
But what else could you do?
Thank goodness some people were kind
They'd try to help you through.

At last you found a great big camp
With tents where you could live;
It still was cold but everyone
Gave all that they could give
To help each other keep the hope
That one day welcome signs
Would show you you'd be safe again
In countries with no mines
Or soldiers with their heavy guns
And eyes as cold as ice
Who'd shout and order you around
And take your little rice.
You children couldn't understand
What made men act this way
It helped to make up stories
Of this country – the UK.

You felt the dread and threat
Of everything in this strange land
For you were weak and wet.
Yet finally you're here with us,
Your friends who've helped you feel
Like happy children once again
No need to hide or steal
You're learning English quick as quick
And even go to school
We might not think you'd say so
But you swear the UK's cool!

Hope In The Eye of The Storm

by Anita Stacey

Time with you.
Oh how sweet is that?
When the world goes mad,
There you are.
In the eye of each storm.

Even as I feel it spinning out of control,
In the horror of it all.
Stories of hope live on.

The Beacon Of Hope by Gabriel Udensi

Trapped in the dungeon of darkness
Forsaken in the pit without water
Deserted at the desert of sorrows
Besieged by wild wicked wolves
Ambushed by merciless leopards
Blood thirsty dragons hovering on the horizon

Ah! Which way to go?
Where shall help come from?
Has the end come?
Any hope of deliverance?

Oh! See the chariots of the Lord's Army
An indomitable and invincible troop
Decelerating on the wings of mercy and grace
With trumpets of hope
And sceptres of deliverance
Seeking for the hopeless
To deliver them from the dungeons of darkness;
From the waterless pits
From the deserts of sorrows
From the caves of hopelessness

As they sound the trumpets of hope
And stretched forth the sceptres of deliverance;

Great light flooded the horizon
The darkened dragons driven away
Prison gates opened
Chains being broken
Captives freed and delivered
Beacon of hope being illuminated

Sing, Sing, Sing
Dance, Dance, Dance
Rejoice, Rejoice, Rejoice
For you are now being surrounded
By songs of deliverance

Never again shall you be ashamed
Never again shall you be disgraced
Never again shall you be forsaken
Never again shall you be hopeless

For on Mount Zion,
The Hill of the Lord
Is your Beacon of hope, established eternally
And its light, shall illuminate continually.

Houses of Hope

By Emma Major

As the world explodes
Houses of Hope develop
Refugees Welcome

Hope in the light

By Basel Basel

What a great day when we get credit
thanks to you it gives us hope
hope in the light of power outages
and the hard times we are experiencing

The Snows of Arsal

by Rachel Summers

The snows of Arsal fall soft and deep
Weighing heavy on the roof of the tent
Above the family fast asleep
Waiting for phone credit to be sent.
Crowded in, twenty-eight to a room
Dreaming of well loved faces of home
Temporary barracks as close as a tomb
Temporary cessation of right to roam.
Awake in the night I feel so alone
An ache for the world heavy on my chest
I live in a city with my friends in my phone
Lockdown's so hard but I know I'm so blessed.
I give thanks to be given this opportunity
To be part of the phone credit community.

We Wait With Hope

By زهرة البنفسج Zahrat

بين صخور عرسالٍ وتجمع الخيم ننتظر لأمل ننتظر
تلك الحظة هل حقاً ستأتي شكرا لمشاركتكم لنا بتلك
لحظات أتمنى السعادة لجميع

Between the rocks of Arsal and the gathering of tents,
we wait with hope,
we wait for that moment,
will it really come,
thank you for sharing with us those moments,
I wish happiness to all

Nameless by Judith Lowans Thurley

it is a nameless pain.
aloneness knows nothing of its own name.
i am empty as a child's bed
and despair is the long night.

far from home
in this my home town.

home might be
the harsh light
of a star's
distant pin
or some burnt stump
of twisted whin
i can only try to imagine
somewhere
out in the dark
in the rain.

i walk years.

there must be a hollow
a dip in earth
that would cradle me.
stop. stoop. hold
the exquisite cold
of a stone to my temple: sleep!
lie down in a gully of rock
among stones
and let the creeping tide
stonepocket me deep.

Behind the Border by Mus Ap

Join me in this group
come hear it from a refugee
I'm going to post on it
I can't stop till I cross the sea

Jump in the water be free
or come and live behind the border with me

I heard you looking
To cross the chain
Blue tent
Wireless phone
I'll wait for my top-up
until the sun is rising

Jump in the water be free
or come and live behind the border like me.

Hope by Jim Cameron

I'm an artist and street artist

I have created this painting, "Hope", with spray paint and acrylic on canvas.

Refugees Fleeing

by Emma Major

Refugees fleeing
Desperately leaving
Everything
Everything!
Taking only what they can carry
Can you imagine?
What would you put in a bag?
A suitcase
For your whole family
I bet you struggle with holiday packing
And this is most likely
For EVER

Women
Children
Elderly
Disabled
Leaving suddenly
Separated from family
Lives in catastrophe
As their men go to war

This is the reality
Of life as a refugee
And yet politically
They're seen as....
Greedy
Needy
Unworthy
Disgustingly

How dare we!
This could be
You or me
By luck of our birth
We live in safety
Work professionally
Whilst doctors and nurses
Teachers and engineers
Flee from their lives
To futures unknown
The least we can do
Is open our doors
And offer new homes
In safety

Poem For The Lost by Sarah Sansbury

I can't - just can't -
look at the photos.
I can't - just can't -
believe that
this brave young man,
this sweet daughter,
this handsome teen
didn't conquer the water
to live their dream,
but instead
lie dead.
What a cost
Immune now to all dangers
they lie, forever lost
to loved ones
and to strangers.
I can't - just can't -
say nothing, scroll away
from the page,
get on with my day,
swallow the rage,
the unthinkability,
the tears that flow for
life's fragility.
I will - just will -
yell it
care it
whisper it
weep it
wear it
living in sadness,
mourning the madness,
becoming fire and fight;
for there is no doubt:
in our hearts, their light
will never go out.

Exodus of Heartbreak

By Emma Major

Beyond calm yellow cornfields
Look at the mess we've created
Anger and jealousy rain down
Lives obliterated

Can we undo damage
Hatch fresh opportunities
Watered by rivers of tears
Mothering over politics

Developing fellowship
Forget moans of yesterday
Echoing intimacies
Discovering similarity

Exodus of heartbreak
A spontaneous journey
Towards a roar of welcome
Beyond political immorality

In Homs I have a house

By Walid Alzane وليد الزين

In Homs I have a house
I have land
I have people
And neighbours
I have a school in the neighbourhood where I left my childhood
And my dreams
And papers in which I wrote that these people are brothers to me
I have a mother like the rest of humanity
I yearn for her laugh and long for her touch
I miss her warm voice
My mother's voice is my home
And my father's face and it's features which are tired of the world
As if all of life is sadness
I whispered to him as he slept in pain
Until he was stolen by his sleep
I am from Homs
Where all of my companions died in silence
I was left on my land with nothing except for the remains of my children
And the blood of those who were once there
In my home which no longer belonged to me
Bats and crows inhabited it after me
There is no safe corner; no roof and no walls
And the people of the neighbourhood, where are they?
What do you know, Oh exile, where are they now?
Does death have a title?
In Homs I had a house
I had land
I had people
And neighbours
In Homs I knew love in all it's sincerity
But you will reject all who came to live under the charity of those who's lives they once inhabited

Views of Arsal

by Mahmod Satof

Isn't this beautiful

by Abu Ayman Al-Kin

هذه ليست لوحة فنية جميلة هذا جليد على احد الخيم بمخيمات عرسال داخلها اطفال
ونساء بعد ماوصلت درجة الحرارة -10 ليل مبارح .شكراً لكم على دعم هذه المخيمات
برصيد الهاتف لنبقى على تواصل مع العالم ولطلب المساعدة عند الضرورة

This is ice on one of the tents in Arsal camps with children and women inside.
The temperature reached -10 last night.
Thank you for supporting these camps with your phone credit,
so that we can stay connected to the world
and ask for help when necessary.

The Reality of Arsal Teacher's Camp by Abu Ayman Al-Kin

هذه الصورة من المخيم الذي اسكنه اسمه مخيم المعلمين في بلدة عرسال اللبنانية فيه 60عائلة تعيش اسوء الظروف
بسبب الحرب بسوريا اطلق عليه اسم مخيم المعلمين لان معظم ساكنيه معلمين واساتذة مدرسة ومعظمهم يحملون
شهدات عليا مثل الماجستير والدبلوم ويتكلمون لغات هنا درجة الحرارة تصل ل 15درجة تحت الصفر ليلا ولايوجد بيننا
وبين المحيط بنا سوا شوادر من الناليون الوضع الاقتصادي منهار تماماَ اكثر الاشخاص لايستطيعون تامين طعامهم
والتدفئة لخيمهم طبعاَ وانا منهم . الحقيقة مجموعة ائتمان الهاتف ساعدت الكثيرين بتامين الاتصالات وطلب المساعدة
عند الضرورة بسبب العجز عن تامين ثمن باقة الاتصالات ولانترنيت بسبب ارتفاعها هنا بالبنان التي تعد من اغلى
بالبلدان بثمن الاتصالات .ان كان هذا مفيد سوف ارسل لكي المزيد من الصور وبعض مانواجهه من مصاعب هنا .شكراَ
لك على اهتمامك .صديقك ابو ايمن الكنج .واعطيك كل الاذن بالتصرف وكتابة مارسله لكي على مسوؤليتي الشخصية

This is Teachers' Camp in the Lebanese town of Arsal
60 families live in the worst conditions because of the war in Syria.
It is called the Teachers' Camp because most of its residents are teachers.
Most people hold higher degrees such as masters and diplomas
Most people speak many languages.

The temperature here reaches 15 degrees below zero at night.
There is nothing between us and those around us except for some of the cables.
The economic situation is completely collapsing.
Most of the people cannot secure food or heat for their tents, I am one of them.
The phone credit group has helped many in securing communications and asking for help when necessary
due to the inability to afford the communications packages in Lebanon.

Watching Injustice

by Emma Major

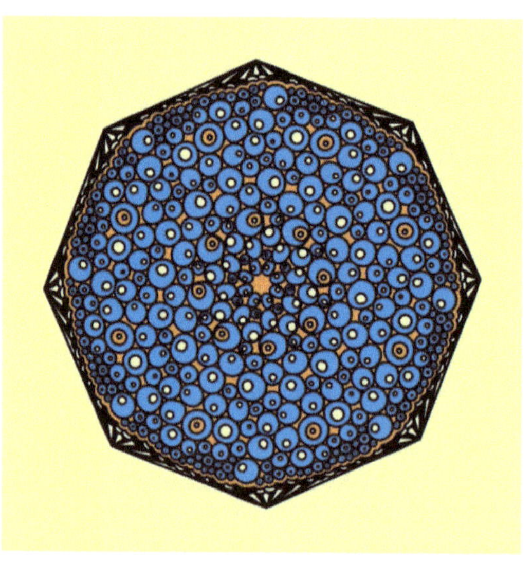

Watching Injustice
Seemingly unmoved by pain
It is inhumane

Fleeing with nothing
Thousands of families
Begging for safety

Reality hits
Selfishness governs the world
How do we change this?

They are refugees
Not economic migrants
It could be me. You.

Close To The Bone

By Judith Lowans Thurley

You find a mark on his inner thigh
just above the knee.
Finger its full-moon smallness.

He rolls over, shocks you
with an explosion of scar tissue
three inches across
at its starburst tips
and nearer the buttock
by a good half-thigh.
He says he was lucky —
it missed the bone, the artery,
on its journey up and through.
Danny got hit in the stomachn
one night down at the youth club:
different story.

You hear of the i.d. parade,
the setting aside of crutches
to approach and touch the man.
How sunglasses are a feeble disguise
for a child murder witness.

Then the death threat,
his mammy weeping,
armed police at the sitting room window.
The hurried sending away
to boarding school across the border,
for his own good.

You come to understand at least this:
that you must not touch that place
on the back of his thigh;
that drink kills the pain;
that a bullet's exit wound
is where it hurts.

From the heart of Arsal

by Mahmod Satof

من قلب عرسال، شكراً لكم ولكل من ساهم ويساهم في مساعدة اللاجئين حول العالم
بفضلكم، نحن نستطيع التواصل مع أهلنا وأقاربنا اللاجئين في مختلف دول العالم شكراً لكم

Thank you to everyone who has contributed and is contributing to help refugees around the world. Because of you, we can communicate with our refugee family and relatives in different countries of the world.

In all the languages of the world

by Nader Mohammed Sadek

Tráthnóna maith do chách, i dteangacha uile an domhain agus i ngach brionna grá. Ba mhaith liom buíochas a ghabháil leat ó chroí. Go raibh maith agat as do chuid ama. Go raibh maith agat as do chabhair. Maolaíonn do chabhair an phian agus an deacracht a bhaineann le cumarsáid a dhéanamh le tuismitheoirí.

Draíocht na hÉireann agus mo mhianta

In all the languages of the world
and in all the meanings of love
I would like to say thank you from the heart.
Thank you for your time.
Thank you for your help.
Your help relieves the pain and the difficulty
of communicating with our parents.

View of Lesvos New Camp
by Chapirot Tekasala

I'm Your Captain by Mus Ap

when you feel like you survived from the war
that feeling is really cool
when you act like you know how to swim
but in fact you don't know
when you said that you love me
and you know anything i used to love
they don't exist anymore
like my girl, my boat and also my tent
I just want you to know
I'm really upset man
all the people I know
what is going on ?

Hannah helps me sing my song
"I'm your captain and you are my immigrant
I'll sail you to safety
sing it
I'm your immigrant you are my captain
I promise you to not let it sink to the depths"

Refugees Welcome

By Emma Major

My heart breaks seeing the news of people dieing in the English Channel
desperately trying to find safety.
My anger rises as rich nations debate who should accept refugees
whilst people die.
My fear increases as I hear people's fear about vulnerable people
with nothing.
My hope fades as I realise humanity is selfish.
Then my faith builds as I find groups of people who care enough to act.
And I cry knowing it's never going to be enough
But I can only do what I can do.
So I pray knowing that God can find a way.

Who Is The Teacher Here?

By Helen Schwake

The lines blurred.
They were from Eritrea and Albania.
And Ghana and Guinea and Syria.
And Ethiopia, Algeria, Kosovo and Morocco.
And Germany.
And England.
They were here for a German class. So it said on the door.
They were safe now.
There was no shooting, no bombs.
They didn't have to hide their thoughts.
They had food and a bed.
They were lonely.
They were far from home. But not alone.
They were black, white, Catholic, Muslim, Orthodox,
Old, young, responsible for families, breaking out on their own.
They were professionals, craftsmen, laborers, students.
They were frustrated, disillusioned, impatient to get on with their lives.
They were worried about those left behind, would they see them again?
They were out of their comfort zone.
They had to dig deep.
Set an example for their children.
Be good ambassadors of their country.
Be thankful for their good fortune.
Good fortune.
Their country was in tatters.
They were alive. They sometimes wished they were not.
Then the music began. A weary icebreaker. Awkward moment as everyone held hands.
Then smiles as 25 people from all over the world tried and failed to step in time.
Something passed through the room from hand to hand.
Community, acceptance, hope.
Who is the teacher here?
The lines blurred.

Our Hearts

by ام ثامر سلام Am Thamir Salam

وتستحق قلوبنا أن تحمل على كفوف من الحُب
ونستحق نحن ألا نهون أو يستهان بنا

Our hearts deserve to be carried on the palms of love
and we deserve not to be underestimated

Observed

By شكرااا الكم Emad Emad

Thank You

by محمد ابو منذر Mohammed Abu Munther

Siraj Eyad Abdul-Al

By Judith Lowans Thurley

aged only 8, of Khan Younis,
I stood on the steps of Broadcasting House
and upheld your name for the cameras.

I pressed your name against my breast
as if that might succour you,
as if that might halt the missile,
as if that might unmake of rubble your home.

Siraj Eyad Abdul-Al,
aged only 8, of Khan Younis,
when we posted the thousand beloved names
of your dead neighbours
on the wall of Broadcasting House
saying them aloud,
chanting justice,
crying STOP! -
we might as well have been
talking to the wall.

Siraj Eyad Abdul-Aal,
aged only 8, of Khan Younis
I wish your mother to know
that I am still saying your name,
even here, even now.

Sunflowers

Painting by Judy Foulsham

Lines of Life by Zahrat

By زهرة البنفسج

I wish I could draw the lines of my life
as I draw them with a sewing machine
and prove colorful happiness
and not put any state of misery in it
only happiness.

Oh God, I ask you for successive happiness that was not planned

Life Is A Beautiful Dream

by Judith Lowans Thurley

life is a beautiful dream
and my son is on top of the hill
waving his arms
not quite in silhouette
for it is still just light
and behind him
the great light of the sky
and the sky arches
over him and over me
and behind me the jostling sea
and carving into the sea
that golden curve of fields and trees

a lean-to and huddle
of hawthorn and whin

the Point

feel the sea's restlessness
inhale the sea's perfume
her seaweed baths
her pebble garlands

today
the universe is a shimmering bay
between two juts of land
and beyond them
a cove
another point
and beyond that

a moment like this is eternity
where even the guttural
the banal
are an echo
of the passion of heaven
and when robin and blackbird
sing
and children's voices
chime and drift
on the salty air
we are already in heaven
and my son is on top of the hill
waving to me
against the light of the sky
and life is a beautiful dream.

Left by Julia Hill

Left their husbands, parents, children and family
Left their beds, belongings and homes
Left their friends, meeting places and communities
Left their schools, workplaces, livelihoods
Left their traditions, towns and cities, country' borders

They didn't want this: they didn't ask for it

Carrying always the heavy burden of loss in their hearts silently,
As they risk the perils of the journey
To a new country, a new people, a new life
In the hope of refuge and peace

Will you and I leave a few comforts to help clothe, feed and welcome a refugee?

Wishes for you by Helena Lyon-Shaw

Lately I've been dreaming of rebirth
Of the way I wanted it to be
Containing my wishes and hopes
Of a tender and present moment of joy

Now to think that so many women
With the same hopes and dreams
From that first butterfly flutter
Will need to abandon that hope

That sense of safety, gone
With a sky that is on fire
A woman's womb housed you all
Her pain gave life to you
And now you destroy her dreams?
The rage in my ribcage
What I feel when I imagine the pain
It is not suitable for print

What can I do for you sisters?
I cry when I think of you
Wishing you dreams of rebirth
No one can take that away from you

Starlight Guides

by Emma Major

Starlight guides the way
From focusing on fear
To praying for peace

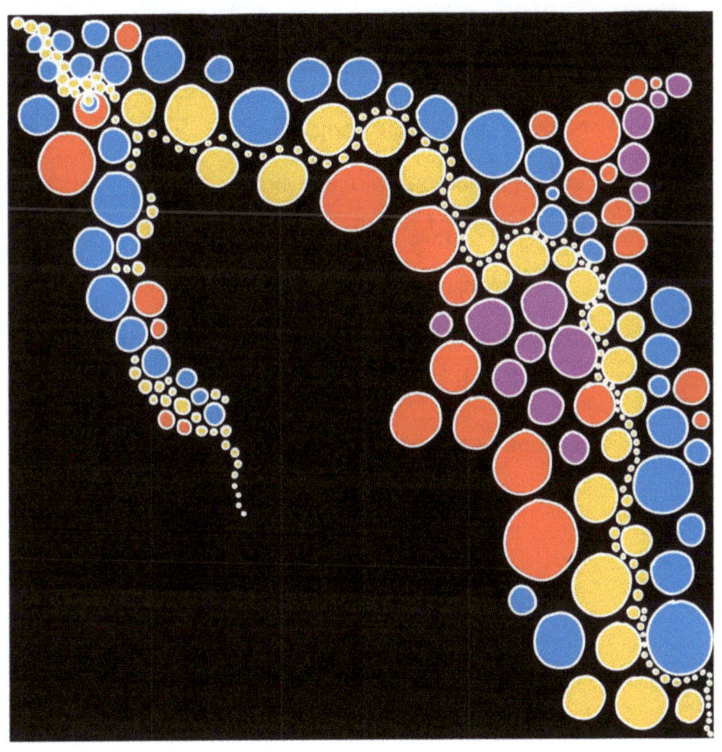

Stars Not Bombs

by Anita Stacey

Do you remember
When I looked into the skies with you
My darling child?
When stars lit up the sky?
I'm sorry that you cannot see them now,
With all the bombs that fly.
I hope that peace comes soon my love,
And hand-in-hand my dear
We'll smile again,
And watch some star, or comet
Light up dark skies so clear.

Retreat by Judith Lowans Thurley

retreat

hours

waves advanced
retreated
when suddenly

i had

strand ocean sky
sand stones cliffs
haze sunset frost
dusk fulmars mist

to myself

i

turned back

tiny as a shell
a pinpoint of light
on inishowen.

Calling for Peace

by Emma Major

Ripples of prayer
Circulating round the world
We're calling for peace

I wish by Mus Ap

She has reached the age of majority
there is no big sister to guide her
she trying to explain me about women thing's
but I can't understand much
I am a man from the sidelines and my culture is limited
my culture is only a boat and migration
but one day I will take you on date in Rome

The smugglers said we will sail tonight
I wish I could put makeup on you tonight
no my baby, you don't need
you are a beautiful girl
most of the people there they do not know the difference
between a migrant and refugee, we are immigrants
no one will notice the makeup on your face
but when we arrive we will buy you a handbag
you will put your things in it
like the beauties

I will tell the people about our trip
and I will complain to the Queen about those who have been going against us
you will give birth in the United kingdom
and you will tell our daughter about our adventures

There will be no more life jacket only a new white dress
and when she grows up
she won't find a Mediterranean Sea to cross
and no English Channel to risk
and I wish we could arrive to safety
to our destination
and leave all the war behind

Eleventh Night by Judith Lowans Thurley

Tonight in A&E
I need no thesaurus:

I'm speechless - breathing
stabs me in the back

and that dark bolus
lodged in my caved-in lung

might any moment obliterate
speech - breath - pulse - thought

My right lung - once beautiful
and intricate as a sponge,

where blood jostled
to exchange gifts with the air,

is a dead space,
clamped shut with pain.

I am alone.
The trolley sides are up.

A no-warning furore
of bawling henchmen

breaks out in the foyer -
shouts ricochet - nurses run.

Terror stalks the corridors
of my head - things not done:

dishes, my unkissed sleeping children,
oblivious, not yet grown.

My funeral.
The imminent unknown.

In my throat,
gasped monosyllables:

nurse -
please -
come!

No Words

by Janene Elise Pike

Kino, Cinema

Diptych Paintings by Kerestey Pavlo, Poem by Yaroslav Futimsky

це війна, це місце називається війна, хотів написати про апокаліптичні
очікування, чекав-вичікував, проснувся, війна.
це диптих, люди дивляться справа наліво, дивляться-мордуються
падає вогонь, огінь-вогонь, комета-ракета.

чи чути тріск, чи далеко видніється зарево-мариво.
комети летять у вашу сторону, де ви дефейсед, де ми?

ци лиця страх, власне не на лицях страх, а саме ці люди страх.
лиця розгортаються і руйнуються, ще до падіння комети-метеору-ракети.

лиця квітнуть смертю і вивертаються, гуснуть і викручуються далі.
спалахи-спалахи.
тріск-тріск.

повітря картини гусне теж, плине плямами, текуча правда, рідка видимість.
всі тіла неначе маса затверділого жиру, проступають очі.

міражі і заховані за металом вітражі, смерть культури, обшиті фанерою
скульптури.
зарево червоне, зарево красиве. диво смерть, муки вичікуванняext

this is war;
this place is called war.

I wanted to write about apocalyptic expectations,
waited-waited,
woke up,
war.

it's a diptych,
people look from right to left, look - a muzzle.
falling fire,
fire - fire,
comet
rocket

whether you hear a crack,
or you can see the glow-dream
in the distance.

comets are flying
towards you,
where are you defeated, where are we?

faces of fear;
actually not faces of fear;
these people fear.

faces unfold and collapse, even before the fall
of the comet
meteor
rocket

faces bloom with death
twist, thicken
and twist further.
flashes - flashes.
crack - crack.

the air of the picture thickens,
flows in spots,
fluid truth,
liquid visibility.
all bodies are like a mass
of hardened fat,
eyes appear.

mirages and stained glass
hidden behind the metal,
the death of culture,
lined with plywood sculptures.

They glow red,
glow beautiful.
miracle of death,
torment of waiting

Sunflower

Painting by Jane Windsor

True Flag

By Sarah Sansbury

Slava Ukraini
Now yellow stands for courage
And blue, for our tears

Mandala by Emma Major

Slav Ukraine

By Michele Thomas

Friday Conga Crew
by Anna Forster

Join the Friday Conga Fun

By Emma Major

Every week thousands of us donate a small amount of money to give phone credit to a refugee or displaced person.
Every tiny amount helps, because added together it is a lot of money.
But the requests are always increasing and the needs are real.
Can you join this amazing cause and allow people to call their families?
It really is the best end to the week.

Acknowledgements

My thanks go to each of the writers, poets, photographers and artists
who have so generously donated their creativity.
I feel honoured to have been entrusted with your stories
and thankful for the friendships that have developed.

Any one of us could become a refugee
Fleeing our homes
At a moments notice
Crossing borders in fear
Travelling into the unknown
Into the darkness
Living in tents
For months
Years
Decades
This is the reality
For over 80 million people
It can feel impossible to help
But we can make a difference
Every book sold, every donation
Every action shines a
Light of Hope

Every penny raised through the sale of this book
will be donated to the charity Phone Credit for Refugees.

www.ingramcontent.com/pod-product-compliance
Ingram Content Group UK Ltd.
Pitfield, Milton Keynes, MK11 3LW, UK
UKHW021841270726
14058UKWH00002B/267

9 781471 714160